HOW TO DRAW
DRAGONS

Mark Bergin

BOOK HOUSE

SALARIYA

Published in Great Britain in MMX by
Book House, an imprint of
The Salariya Book Company Ltd
25 Marlborough Place, Brighton BN1 1UB

5 7 9 8 6 4

Please visit our website at **www.book-house.co.uk**
or go to **www.salariya.com** for **free** electronic versions of:
You Wouldn't Want to be an Egyptian Mummy!
You Wouldn't Want to be a Roman Gladiator!
You Wouldn't Want to be a Polar Explorer!
**You Wouldn't Want to sail on a 19th-Century
  Whaling Ship!**

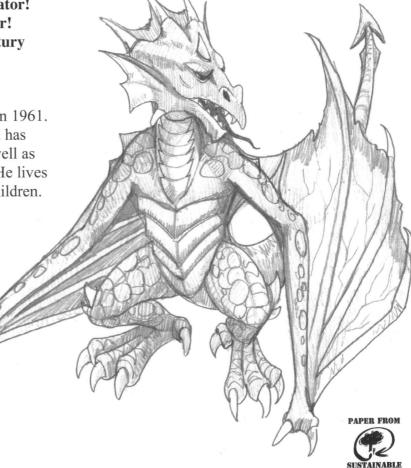

Author: Mark Bergin was born in Hastings in 1961.
He studied at Eastbourne College of Art and has
specialised in historical reconstructions as well as
aviation and maritime subjects since 1983. He lives
in Bexhill-on-Sea with his wife and three children.

Editor: Rob Walker

PB ISBN: 978-1-907184-29-1

A CIP catalogue record for this
book is available from the
British Library.

Printed and bound in China.
Printed on paper from
sustainable sources.
Reprinted in MMXIV.

**WARNING: Fixatives should be
used only under adult supervision.**

PAPER FROM
SUSTAINABLE
FORESTS

Contents

Making a start

Learning to draw is about looking and seeing. Keep practising and get to know your subject. Use a sketchbook to make quick drawings. Start by doodling, and experiment with shapes and patterns. There are many ways to draw; this book shows only some methods. Visit art galleries, look at artists' drawings, see how friends draw, but above all, find your own way.

Drawing materials

Try using different types of drawing paper and materials. Experiment with charcoal, wax crayons and pastels. All pens, from felt-tips to ballpoints, will make interesting marks — you could also try drawing with pen and ink on wet paper.

Silhouette is a style of drawing which mainly uses solid black shapes.

Ink

Lines drawn in **ink** cannot be erased, so keep your ink drawings sketchy and less rigid. Don't worry about mistakes as these lines can be lost in the drawing as it develops.

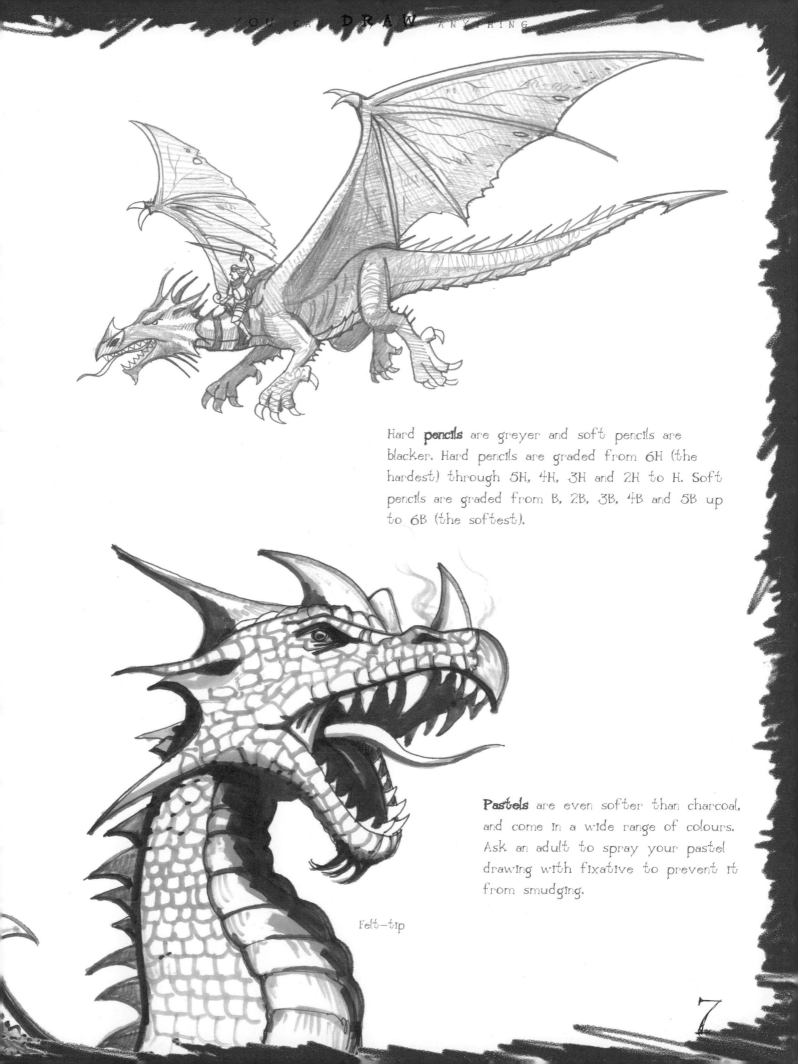

Hard **pencils** are greyer and soft pencils are blacker. Hard pencils are graded from 6H (the hardest) through 5H, 4H, 3H and 2H to H. Soft pencils are graded from B, 2B, 3B, 4B and 5B up to 6B (the softest).

Pastels are even softer than charcoal, and come in a wide range of colours. Ask an adult to spray your pastel drawing with fixative to prevent it from smudging.

Felt-tip

7

Perspective

If you look at any object from different viewpoints, you will see that the part that is closest to you looks larger, and the part furthest away from you looks smaller.

Drawing in perspective is a way of creating a feeling of depth — of showing three dimensions on a flat surface.

The vanishing point (V.P.) is the place in a perspective drawing where parallel lines appear to meet. The position of the vanishing point depends on the viewer's eye level. Sometimes a low viewpoint can give your drawing added drama.

V.P.

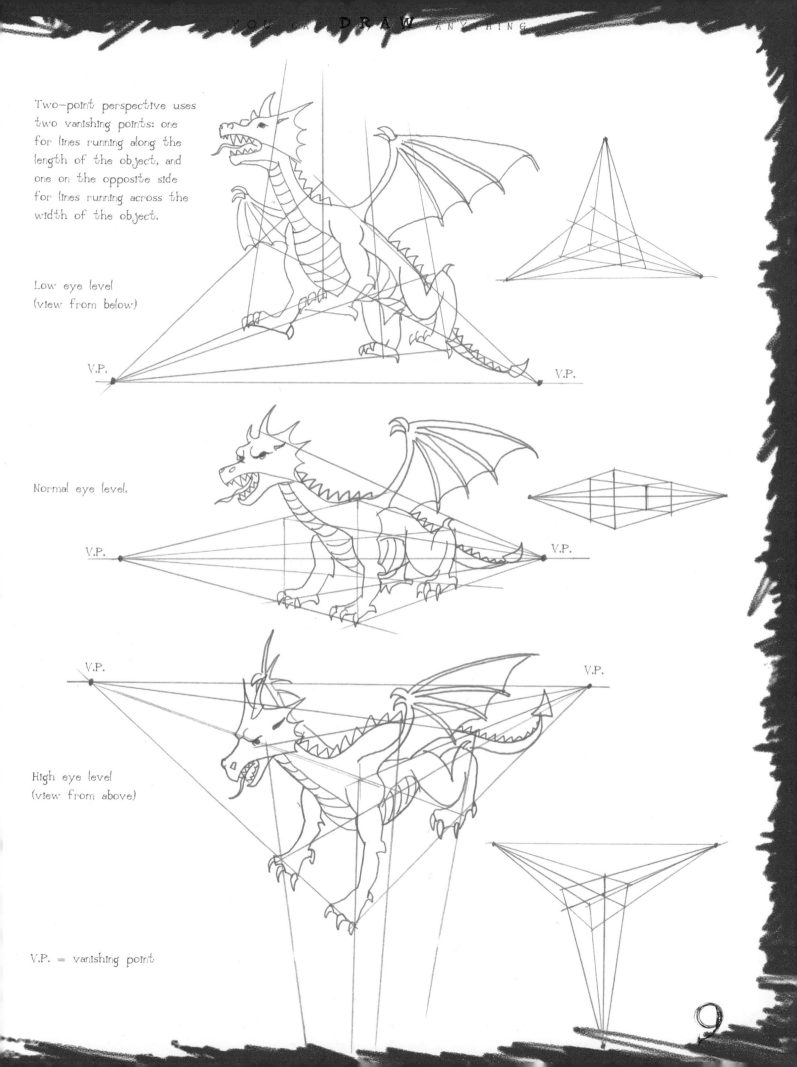

Two-point perspective uses two vanishing points: one for lines running along the length of the object, and one on the opposite side for lines running across the width of the object.

Low eye level
(view from below)

V.P.

V.P.

Normal eye level.

V.P.

V.P.

High eye level
(view from above)

V.P.

V.P.

V.P. = vanishing point

9

References

There are many different types of dragon from numerous cultures around the world. When creating your own dragons you can use these references to help you with your drawing.

The Welsh dragon is the emblem that appears on the Welsh flag.

St. George and the dragon is a famous English story and has been depicted in many ways by different artists.

Chinese dragons are often drawn as long, thin, scaly creatures with four legs and no wings.

A Wyvern is a type of dragon with one set of wings and only two legs.

Give some thought to how many legs and wings you would like your dragon to have before you create it.

Dragon head

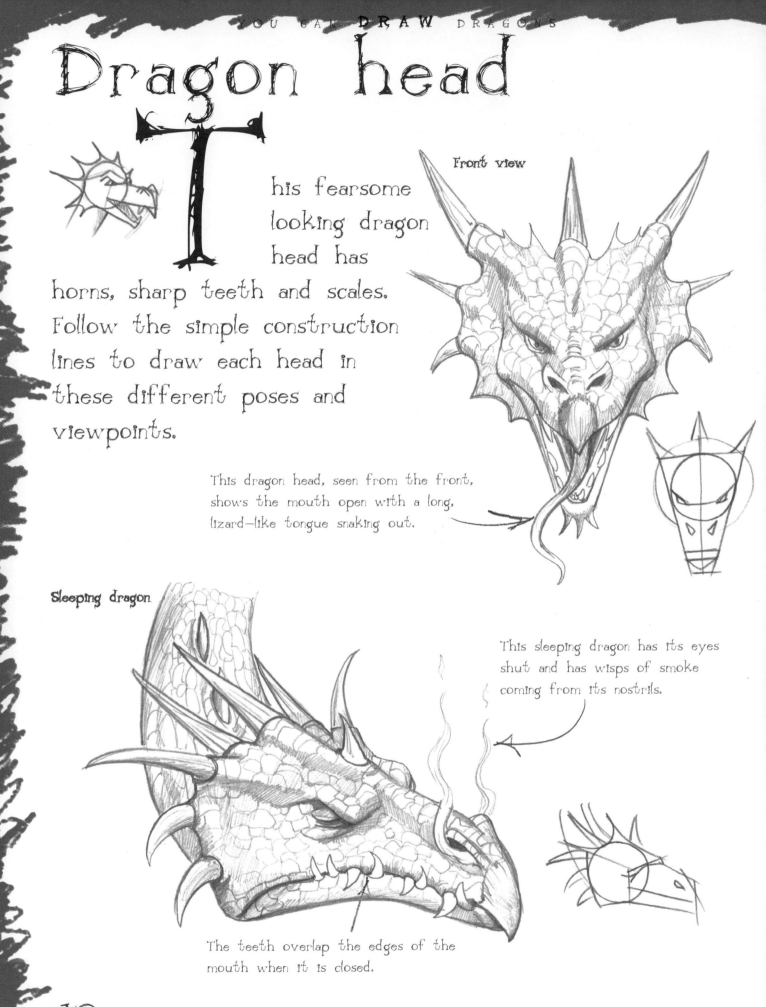

This fearsome looking dragon head has horns, sharp teeth and scales. Follow the simple construction lines to draw each head in these different poses and viewpoints.

Front view

This dragon head, seen from the front, shows the mouth open with a long, lizard-like tongue snaking out.

Sleeping dragon

This sleeping dragon has its eyes shut and has wisps of smoke coming from its nostrils.

The teeth overlap the edges of the mouth when it is closed.

Breathing fire

This dragon is breathing fire! Add curved lines coming out of the dragon's mouth to represent fire.

The dragon's skin is made up of a patchwork of different sized scales.

Fearsome roar

In this drawing the dragon bares all its teeth in a fearsome roar. Make sure the teeth are as sharp as possible.

13

Birth of a dragon

A baby dragon hatches from an egg. Draw the dragon emerging from the cracked egg.

Draw an oval shape for the dragon's head.

Draw two curved lines to indicate the neck.

Draw a large oval for the egg.

Add the basic wing shapes using curved lines.

Draw the beak as a simple shape using straight lines.

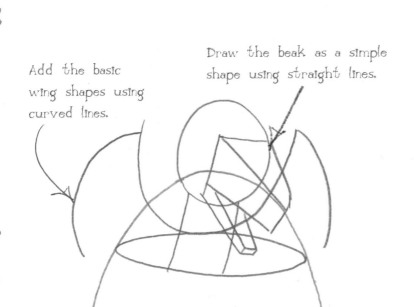

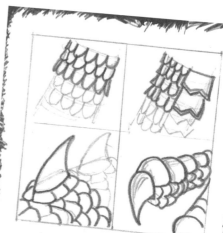

Scales

The dragon's scales overlap each other in rows. You can see the tip of each scale but its base is covered by the one overlapping it.

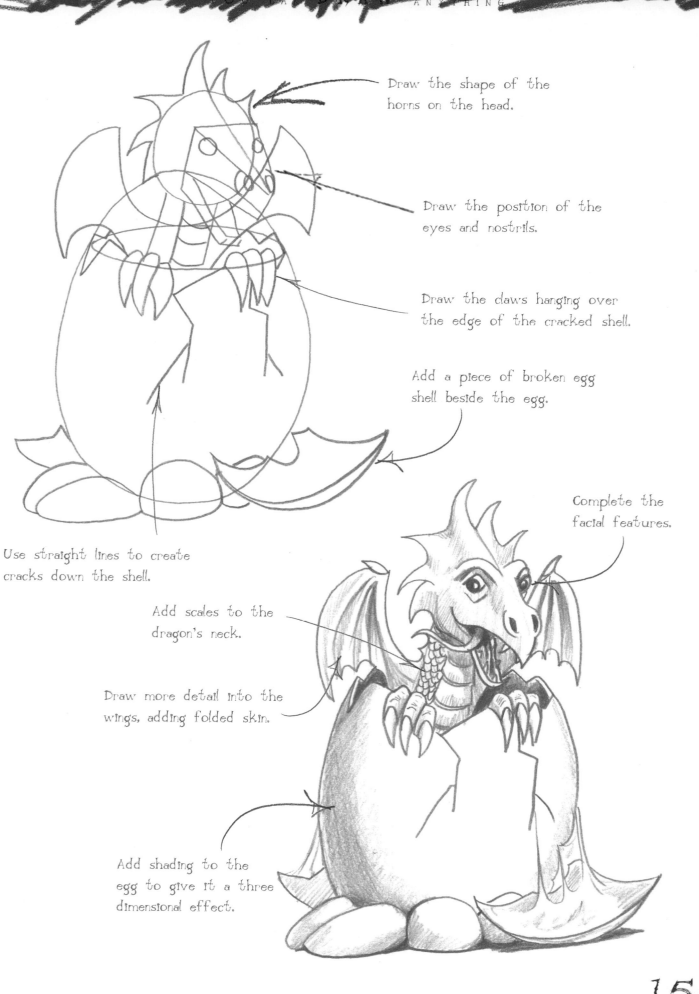

Draw the shape of the horns on the head.

Draw the position of the eyes and nostrils.

Draw the claws hanging over the edge of the cracked shell.

Add a piece of broken egg shell beside the egg.

Use straight lines to create cracks down the shell.

Complete the facial features.

Add scales to the dragon's neck.

Draw more detail into the wings, adding folded skin.

Add shading to the egg to give it a three dimensional effect.

Sleeping dragon

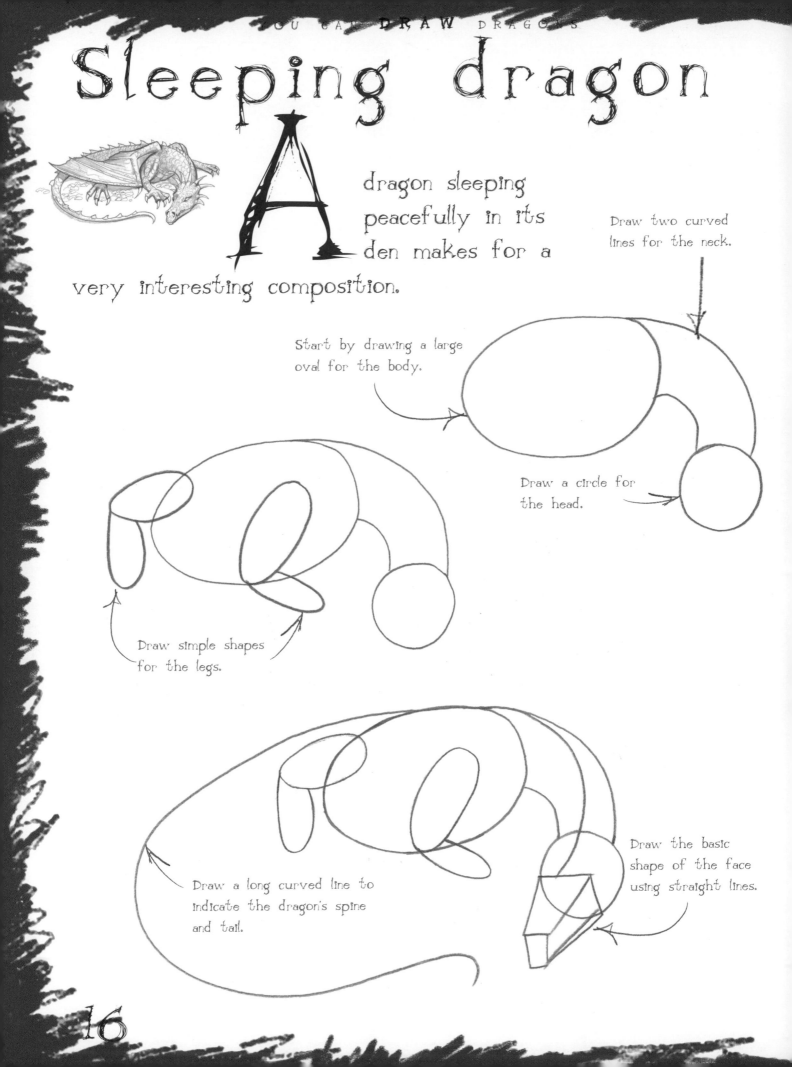

A dragon sleeping peacefully in its den makes for a very interesting composition.

Draw two curved lines for the neck.

Start by drawing a large oval for the body.

Draw a circle for the head.

Draw simple shapes for the legs.

Draw a long curved line to indicate the dragon's spine and tail.

Draw the basic shape of the face using straight lines.

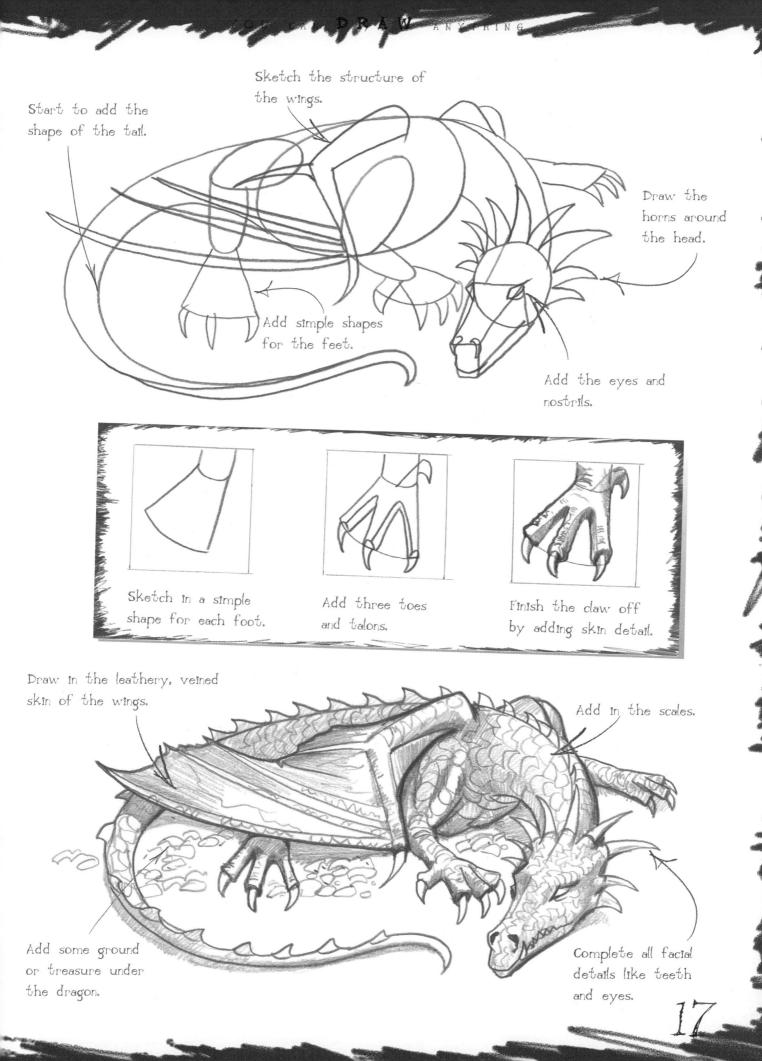

Sketch the structure of
the wings.

Start to add the
shape of the tail.

Draw the
horns around
the head.

Add simple shapes
for the feet.

Add the eyes and
nostrils.

Sketch in a simple
shape for each foot.

Add three toes
and talons.

Finish the claw off
by adding skin detail.

Draw in the leathery, veined
skin of the wings.

Add in the scales.

Add some ground
or treasure under
the dragon.

Complete all facial
details like teeth
and eyes.

17

Fire-breathing dragon

T his fiery dragon blasts its foes with red-hot flames to incinerate them.

Draw a circle for the head.

Draw curved lines to form the neck.

Draw a large oval for the body.

Draw the position and angle of the legs using ovals and curved lines.

Draw the basic shape of the face with straight lines, then position the eyes and nostrils.

Draw a curved line for the tail.

Roughly draw the shape of each foot.

Add horns to the head.

Draw the shape of the wings using curved lines.

Draw small triangles on the feet for the claws.

Add curved lines to complete the shape of the tail.

Draw a curved line to indicate the dragon's belly.

Chiaroscuro

Add dark shading to parts of your drawing for a dramatic effect.

Complete the facial details, like sharp teeth, flaring nostrils and eyes.

Draw the leathery skin covering the wings. Include details such as veins and cracks in the skin.

Draw the flames blasting out of the dragon's mouth using a series of curved lines.

Draw a line of spiked horns running from its neck to its tail.

Draw the scaly pattern of the skin

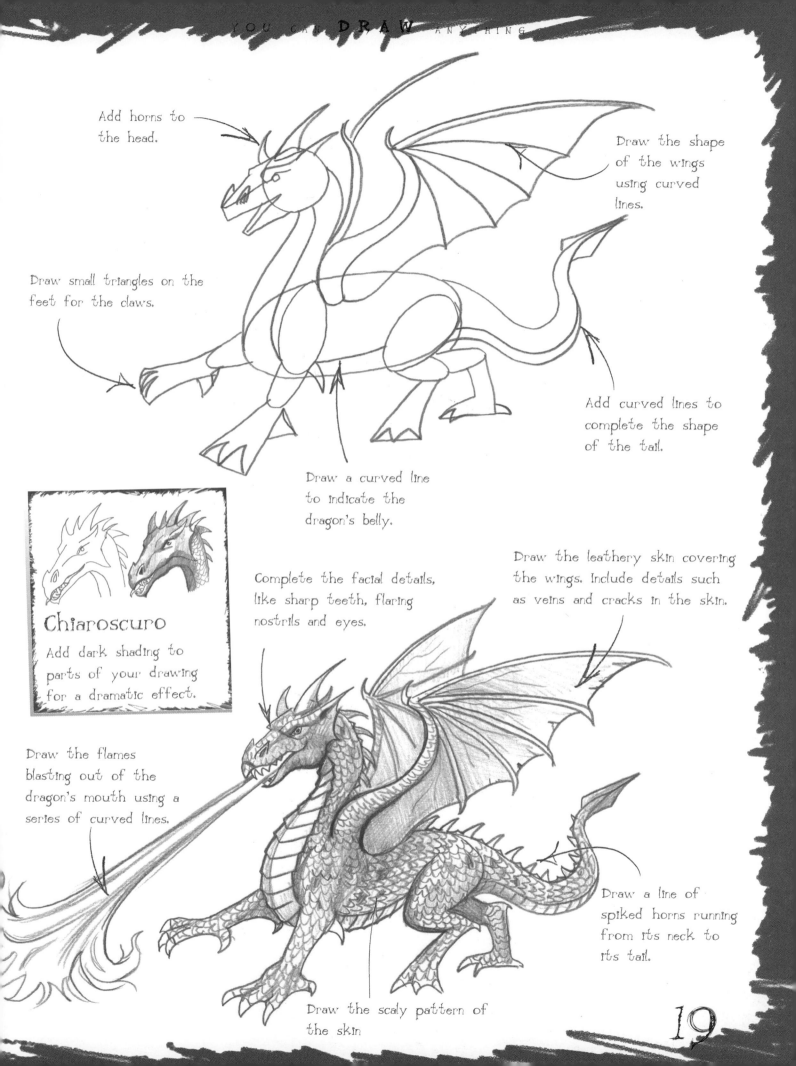

19

The wise dragon

The ancient dragon offers wise advice and insight to those brave enough to ask!

Draw a circle for the head.

Draw curved lines for the neck.

Draw a large oval for the body.

Add the shape of the face using straight lines.

Draw the shape of the legs using ovals.

Draw the main structure of the wings.

Add two long curved lines extending out from the body to become the tail.

Draw semi-circles on the end of each leg to place the feet.

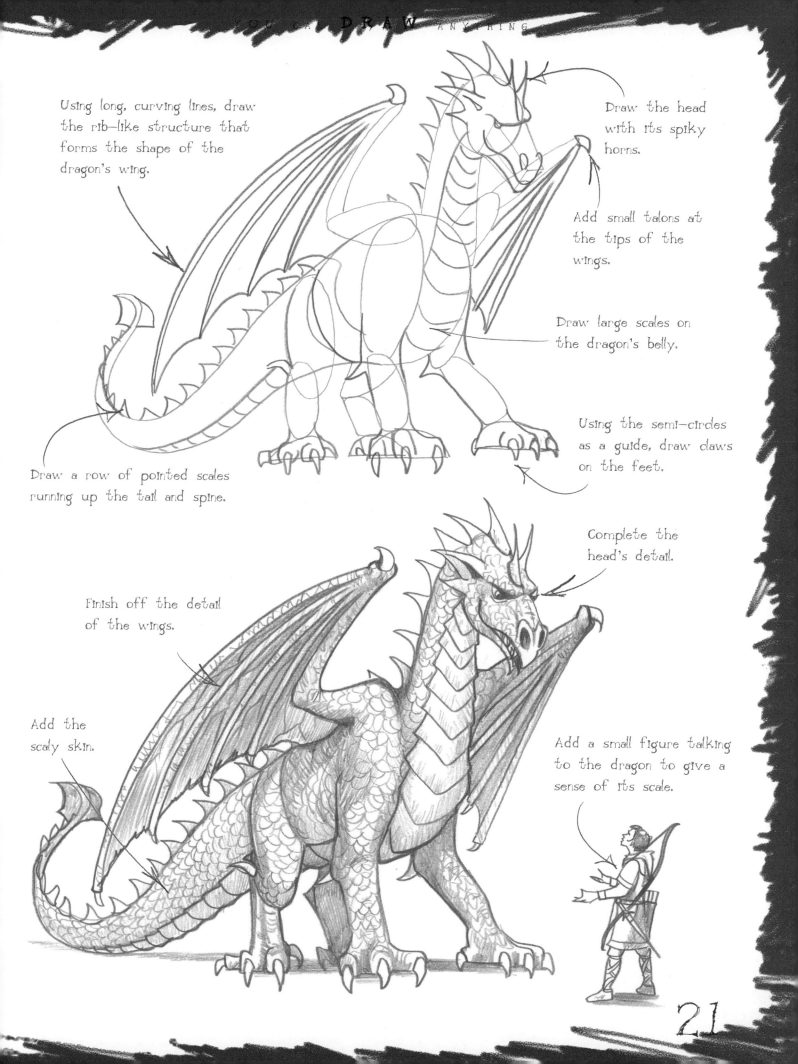

Using long, curving lines, draw the rib-like structure that forms the shape of the dragon's wing.

Draw the head with its spiky horns.

Add small talons at the tips of the wings.

Draw large scales on the dragon's belly.

Draw a row of pointed scales running up the tail and spine.

Using the semi-circles as a guide, draw claws on the feet.

Complete the head's detail.

Finish off the detail of the wings.

Add the scaly skin.

Add a small figure talking to the dragon to give a sense of its scale.

21

Perched dragon

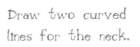

This dragon is perched on a large rock waiting patiently for its next victim to appear.

Draw a circle for the head.

Draw two curved lines for the neck.

Draw a large oval for the body.

Draw in the basic shape of the head.

Draw a curved horn shape for the arm of the wing.

Add two overlapped ovals for the rear leg.

Draw in the front legs using simple shapes.

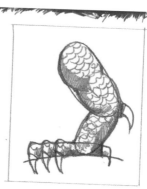

Legs

Remember when drawing the dragon's legs that shading helps define the muscle.

Add horns to
the head.

Draw in a curved line
for the tongue.

Draw a line to
indicate the belly.

Add on the feet
and claws.

Draw curved lines
for the shape of
the wings.

Add details of the dragon's
head, remembering the sharp
teeth and pointed tongue.

Draw two long lines
coming to a point for
the tail.

Draw the leathery veined
skin of the wings. Add
interesting details like
tears and holes.

Draw the rock the dragon
is perched on.

23

Flying dragon

A dragon in flight is a majestic sight. With its powerful wings extended it can fly through the air at astonishing speeds.

Draw a circle for the head.

Draw two lines for the neck.

Draw a large oval for the body.

Roughly draw the shape of the head.

Draw the dragon's four legs.

Add a horn to the head.

Draw long curved lines for the arms of the wings.

Add long curved lines to position the tail.

Wings

Start by drawing the curved arm. Then add spikes splaying out from the top and join the spikes with curved lines.

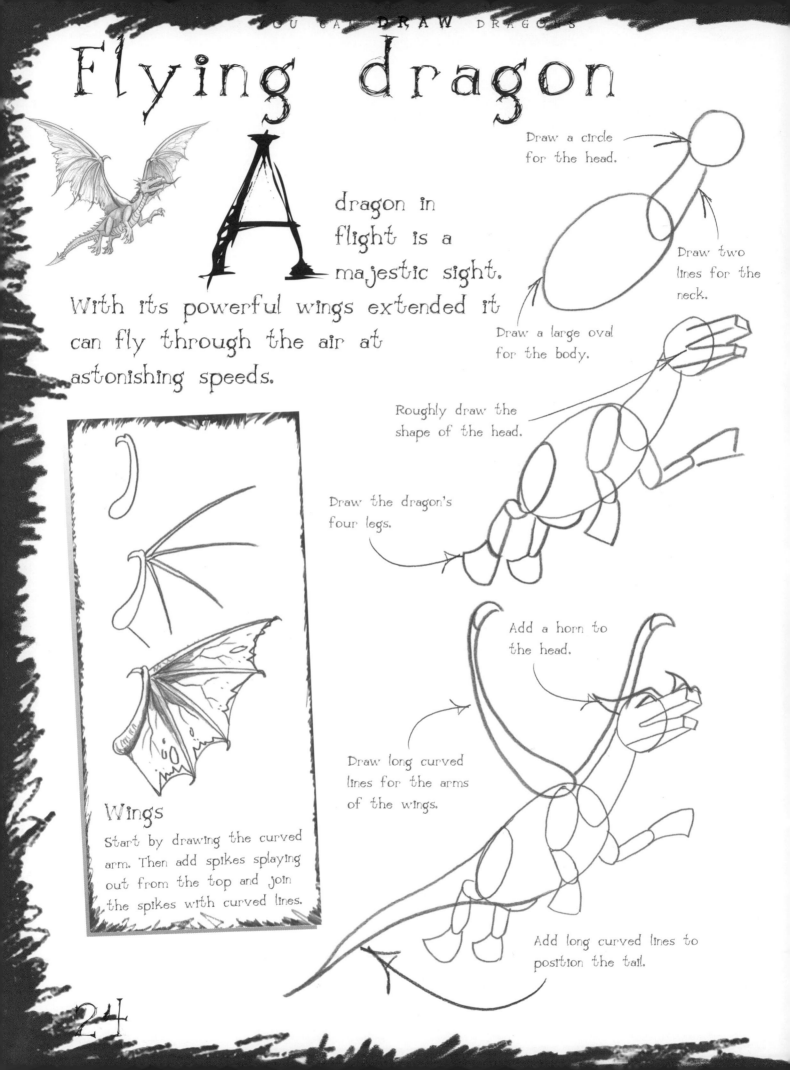

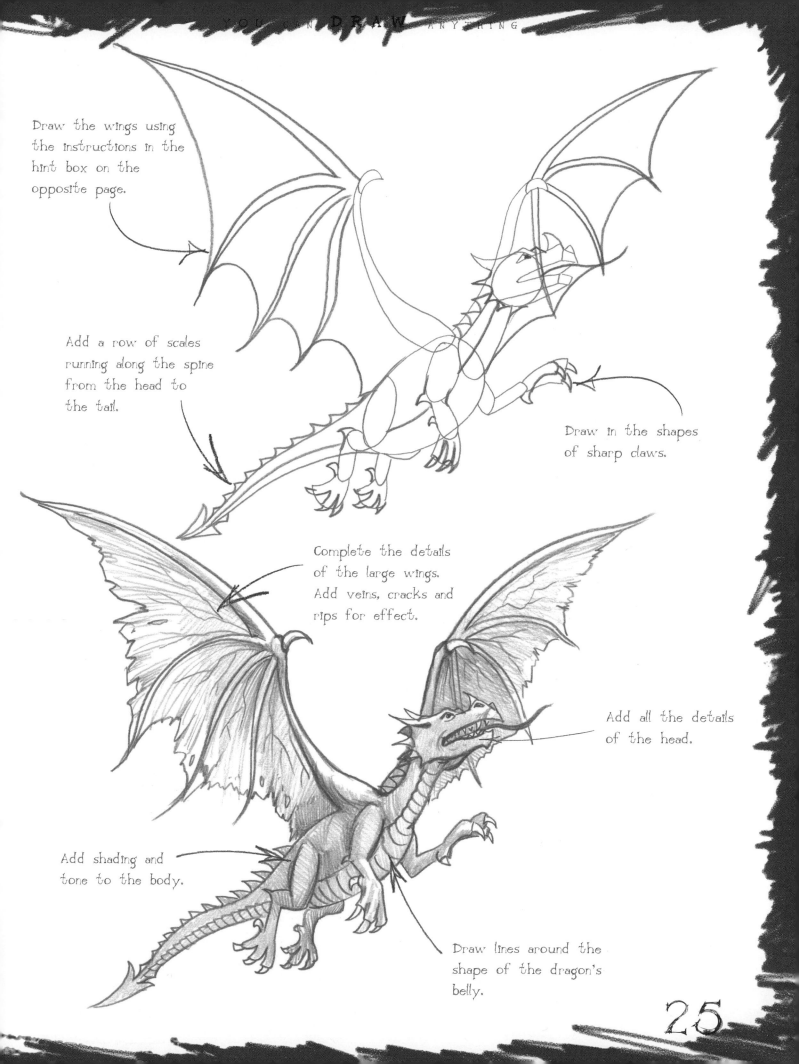

Draw the wings using the instructions in the hint box on the opposite page.

Add a row of scales running along the spine from the head to the tail.

Draw in the shapes of sharp claws.

Complete the details of the large wings. Add veins, cracks and rips for effect.

Add all the details of the head.

Add shading and tone to the body.

Draw lines around the shape of the dragon's belly.

Battling dragons

Two dragons confront one another to do battle in the sky. Who will be the winner in this ferocious fight?

Draw two circles to position the dragons' heads.

Start by drawing two large ovals for the dragons' bodies.

Add long curved lines to each dragon to position the tails.

Draw each dragon's legs, sketching in their shape simply.

Construction lines

Construction lines should always be drawn lightly. That way you can easily erase them when you finish the drawing.

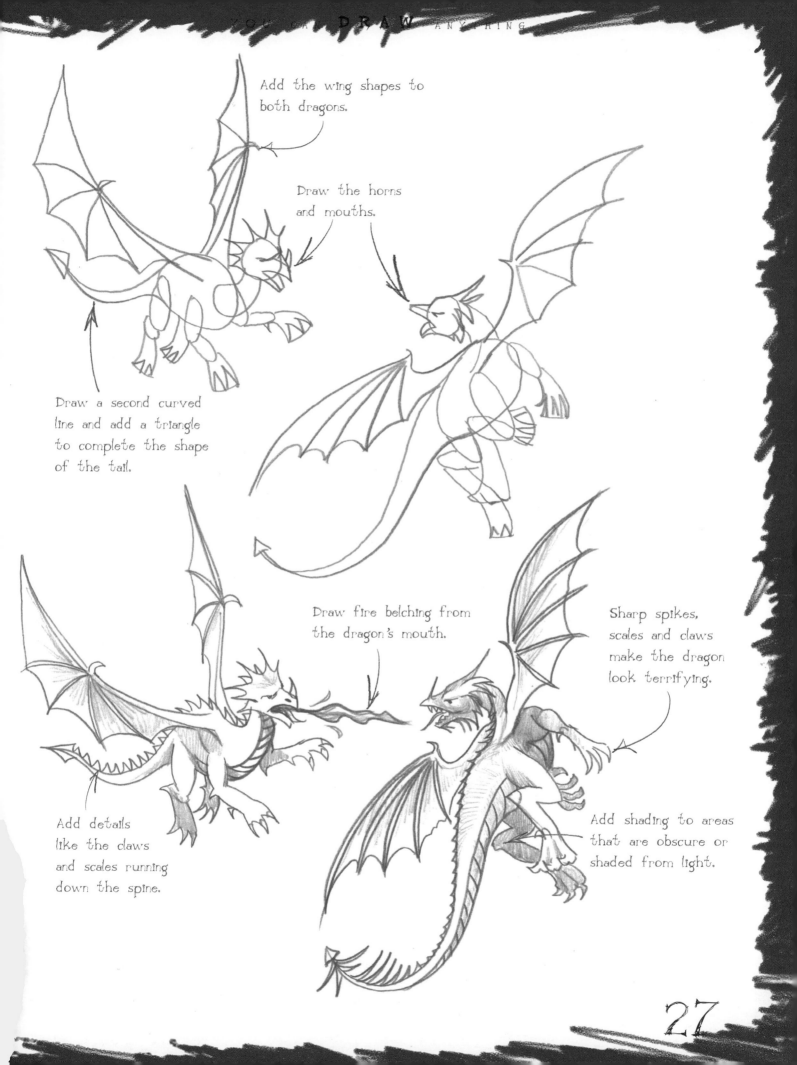

Add the wing shapes to both dragons.

Draw the horns and mouths.

Draw a second curved line and add a triangle to complete the shape of the tail.

Draw fire belching from the dragon's mouth.

Sharp spikes, scales and claws make the dragon look terrifying.

Add details like the claws and scales running down the spine.

Add shading to areas that are obscure or shaded from light.

27

Dragon and slayer

Many tales are told of brave knights who set off to confront a dragon. Will any of these warriors survive the battle ahead?

Start by drawing a large oval for the dragon's body and a smaller one for the head.

Join both shapes with two curved lines for the neck.

Sketch the position of the mouth.

Add the legs using simple curved shapes.

Extend the back of the dragon's head outwards in a fan shape.

Add the eyes, ears, nostrils and tongue.

Sketch the position of the tail with one long curved line.

Roughly draw the shape of each foot.

Draw the dragon's large wings with a series of curved lines.

Add claw shapes to each foot.

Add the scales of the chest and belly.

Complete the shape of the tail with a second long curving line.

Complete the details of the head, including fearsome teeth and spiked nostrils.

Draw small knights fighting the ferocious dragon.

Complete all details, adding shading to all areas with less light.

29

Fire and ice dragons

An intense battle rages in the sky! Two opposing dragons fight above a backdrop of mountains and a solar eclipse.

Draw a circle for each dragon's head and a large oval for each of their bodies.

Add a long curved line for each dragon's tail.

Join the heads to the bodies with curved lines for each dragon's neck.

Roughly sketch the shape of each head.

Draw the position and angle of each of the feet.

Add the leg shapes using ovals.

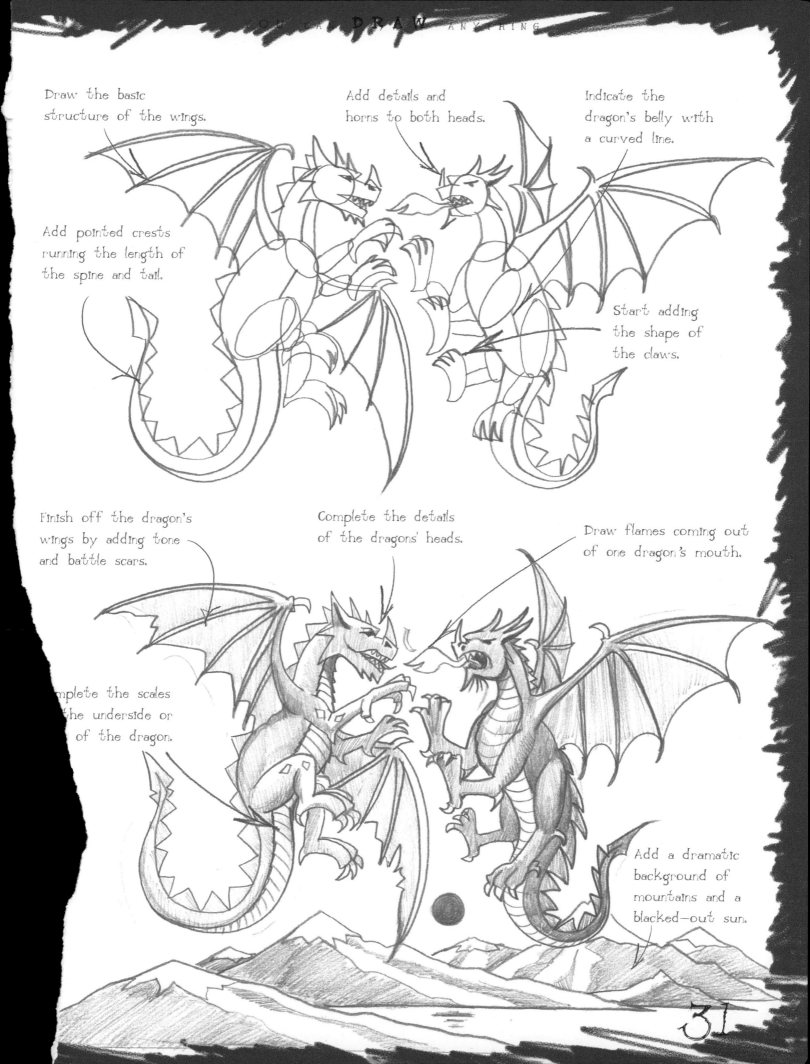

Draw the basic structure of the wings.

Add details and horns to both heads.

Indicate the dragon's belly with a curved line.

Add pointed crests running the length of the spine and tail.

Start adding the shape of the claws.

Finish off the dragon's wings by adding tone and battle scars.

Complete the details of the dragons' heads.

Draw flames coming out of one dragon's mouth.

mplete the scales the underside or of the dragon.

Add a dramatic background of mountains and a blacked-out sun.

31

Glossary

Chiaroscuro The practice of drawing high contrast pictures with a lot of black and white, but not much grey.

Composition The arrangement of the parts of a picture on the drawing paper.

Construction lines Guidelines used in the early stages of a drawing. They are usually erased later.

Fixative A type of resin used to spray over a finished drawing to prevent smudging. **It should only be used by an adult.**

Light source The direction from which the light seems to come in a drawing.

Perspective A method of drawing in which near objects are shown larger than faraway objects to give an impression of depth.

Pose The position assumed by a figure.

Proportion The correct relationship of scale between each part of the drawing.

Silhouette A drawing that shows only a flat dark shape, like a shadow.

Vanishing point The place in a perspective drawing where parallel lines appear to meet.

Index